This is the true story of a little girl and her very important orange shirt.

Six-year-old Phyllis Webstad was as excited to wear her shiny new orange shirt as she was to attend school for the first time. But her first day at the St. Joseph Mission near Williams Lake, BC was nothing like she expected. Her orange shirt was taken away from her, never to be returned.

Since 2013, each year on September 30th, we wear orange to honour the Residential School survivors like Phyllis. We honour their experiences and the experiences of their families. Orange Shirt Day is an opportunity for First Nations, local governments, schools and communities to all come together in the spirit of reconciliation and hope for future generations of children.

It is a day to reaffirm that EVERY CHILD MATTERS.

We mark the end of September because that was the month when children were taken from their homes to go to residential schools. September was described by one elder as the "crying month."

Phyllis is so thankful that children are learning about First Nations history. It is something she learned little about when she was at school. It is important that we know our (and each other's) histories. She is overjoyed that you are taking part and learning the true history of the first peoples of Canada.

For more information on Orange Shirt Day, visit www.orangeshirtday.org

For some families this topic of residential schools is very sensitive and difficult. If you need crisis support please contact Indian Residential Schools Resolution Health Support Program at 1-866-925-4419.

The orange shirt story was translated from English into Shuswap for the purpose of furthering the development of language and culture. Thank you to the translators for their hard work.

Editor : Emma Bullen
Translated to Shuswap: Bridget Dan and Cody William
Project Manager: Teddy Anderson
All Text and Illustrations Copyrighted @ Medicine Wheel Education 2018
Printed in PRC.
ISBN-978-1-989122-01-3
For more information visit www.orangeshirtbook.com OR www.medicinewheel.education

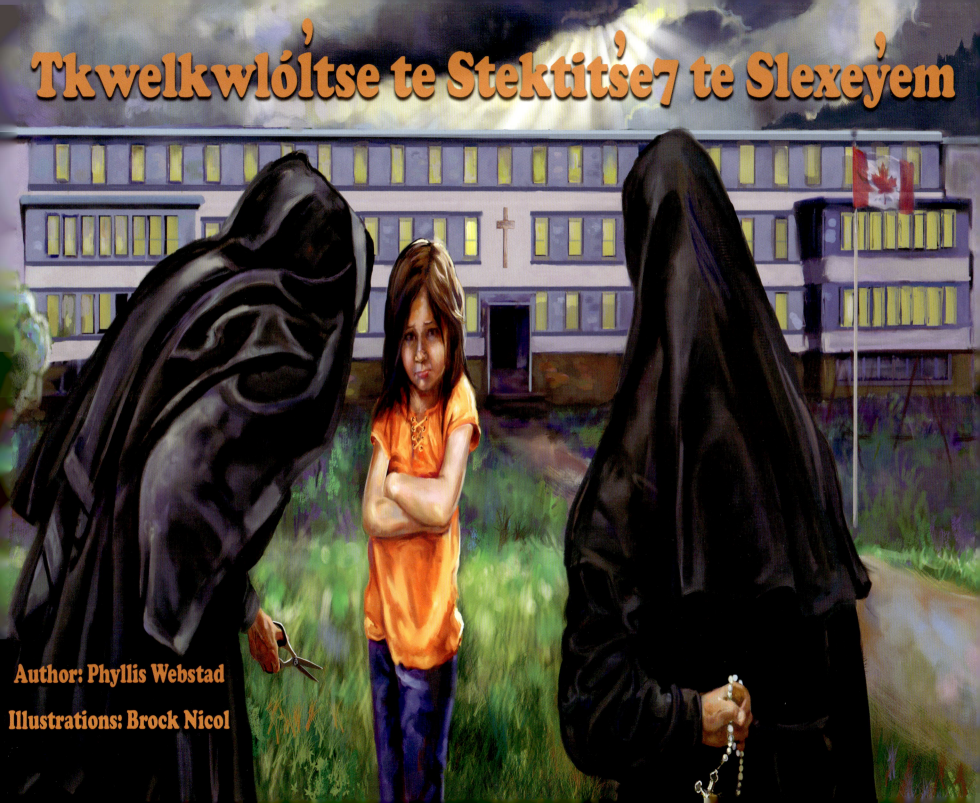

Tkwelkwlóltse te Stektitse7 te Slexeyem

Author: Phyllis Webstad
Illustrations: Brock Nicol

Le k̓woyí7sus re Phyllis, lu7 mut mete Kyé7es ne X̱get̓tém̓, yirí7 re Stswéceḿc X̱get̓tém̓ txeteqs te qelmúcw. Ne tsitscws ta7 k pell tsék̓wsteń ell tek ct̓ekteń ne ck̓emteḿ. Ne Sexqél̓tqeltemc, re m xixéytes, re Phyllis me7 perelc ne csécwmeń qwetśt te séwllkwe te sten ne Kyé7es, re s7íllens stéḿi7 k kulens ne ck̓wéńllqtens ell re speqpéq te sq̓wléwems.

Re Phyllis mete Kyé7es m nes te Setétkwe es yéwems tek sqlélten. M c7íllen te sqlélten ne screpqín ell m cwíkens re s7i7llcw es k̓willems ne s7istk. Ta7 ri7 put k pesecw7ítes k̓eméll ri7 m le7 re swé7ces.

Wes ne twites, cwemcwem lu7 re Phyllis. Ta7 put k scw7it.s k stsmemlt e k̓wellsey̓ses. Ne Pellcwéw̓lemten re sc7itemc te stsmemlt, t̓silem te 7eq̓wi7éwst.s qwetsqwétsets es nests te skul. Re Phyllis w7é7ec te tseklem e yews es cketscusts re newi7s es nests te skul.

Phyllis ta7 put k stukwtukwstem le kwoyí7sus. Kemell re Phyllis westes ey re Kyé7es ell nerí7 ne Kyé7es re tsitscwes re lé7es re xwexwéyt te swet e swe7écs.
Cw7it te qelmúcw ec re tskitscws te Kyé7e es knucwentem ell es ctsenm7íkenteḿ.
Nerí7 re Kyé7e re kitsens re Phyllis re xwexwísteses e sw7ecs.

Re Phyllis le m teq̓mékstes te swucwt ne Pestemllík, k̓ulctem te Kyé7es te kake ne tketscemnúcwes le k̓ultes. Re Phyllis m tsúntmes te Kyé7es te m teq̓mékst te swucwt, nerí7 re tsq̓éy̓es e skuls. Le m Pescwéw̓lemtnes yirí7 te sxeteqs es snests te St. Joseph's Mission Skul.

Nerí7 re Phyllis re sxeteqsts re sq7ists es snests te skul ell e seysests re 7eq̓wi7ews ell re s7i7llcw te stsmemlt. Tsuns e stselxemwílcsts ec k kenems t̓lu7ȷell m tsut me7 k̓úlem tek stemtmet.

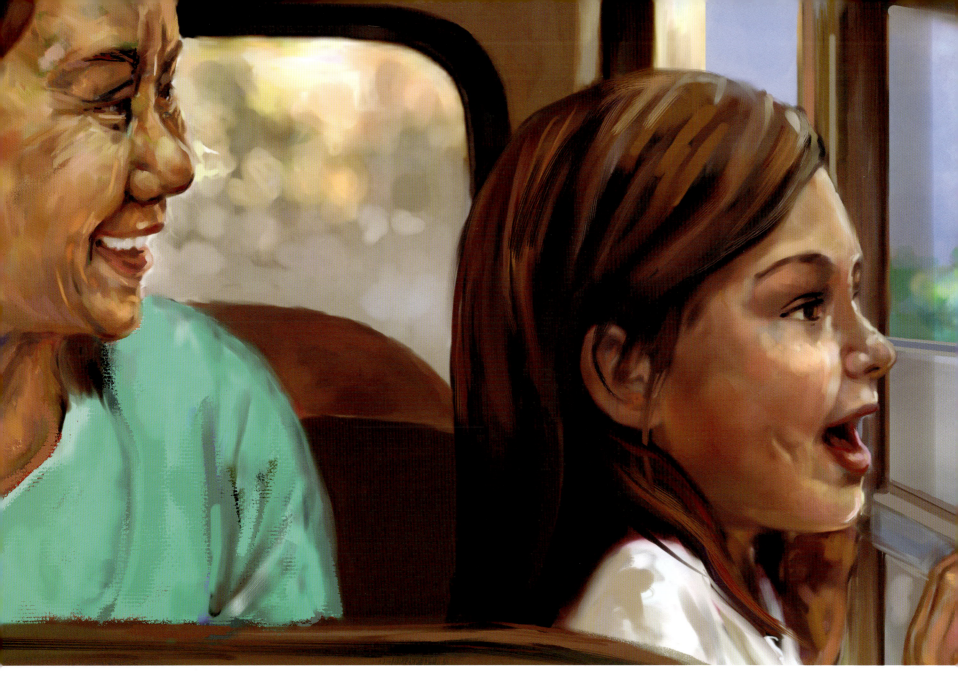

Ey ne sxeteqs te skuls, Re Kyé7es m kwens re Phyllis te tegwn e stewcts tek tsitslem te stektsítṡe7. Ta7 k pellnexúlecws ell re m neses te tegwn ri7 me7 clleqelc ne qwiqwyéẁll te nexúlecw ts7emtstem te "stage".

Nerí7 m q7ises re m neses te tegwen! Tkllúne re sweytsins re stage ne tsecyemes ell ckesúlecw re cucwell. Ta7 k sqe7sts m letwílcwes re st7eks ell m tekukwes. Phyllis setsex skempéllecw ell wiktses re clecews te cucwell ne t7ekwes.

Re tegwn kllúne re sketsctsíns ell put e then k qeqélmucw ell nexnexúlecw.
Ctetuméllcw te tegwnmentem ell c7e7llnellcw ne sc7illnemc.
Nekú7 te ctuméllcw pell tsiqw ell piq te tsrep stslucw skempéllcw. Re Phyllis m tspiqwsts ec te cwlepes ell m tsut thenesénke wes k t7ekwes re stsegwtsúgw.

Re Kyé7es m kwens re Phyllis te c7ellnellcw. M lleqelc neri7 ne sclleqelcten, pell k̓woyí7se te csetsinten. Re m ctséq̓mimentmes nerí7 k sqlew̓ me7 setsinem ri7. Re Phyllis m sulltimc te cwenwenstsíllen tek cselilt te ú7se, ell le m tskitsctmes lu7 tśílem te cgweswespus. Wel tspiqwestem re Phyllis te ú7ses ne syeltes, ta7k stselxemstes me7 kests e 7illenses. – Kyé7e re ú7sests kumtus re tspeltsmett.s

Le m wetsínes re Kyé7e m kwens re Phyllis te ctuméllcw, cw7it nerí7 re stsyex ell syeksten. Re Phyllis m k̓wenem te gwellgwéllt tkwelkwlółtśe te stektítśe7, te stlk̓entet.s ne tek̓mélests. Tsekwtsek̓w ell tseqwtsúq̓wt lu7.
Le7 re sptínesmens re stektítśe7s ell e snests te skul.

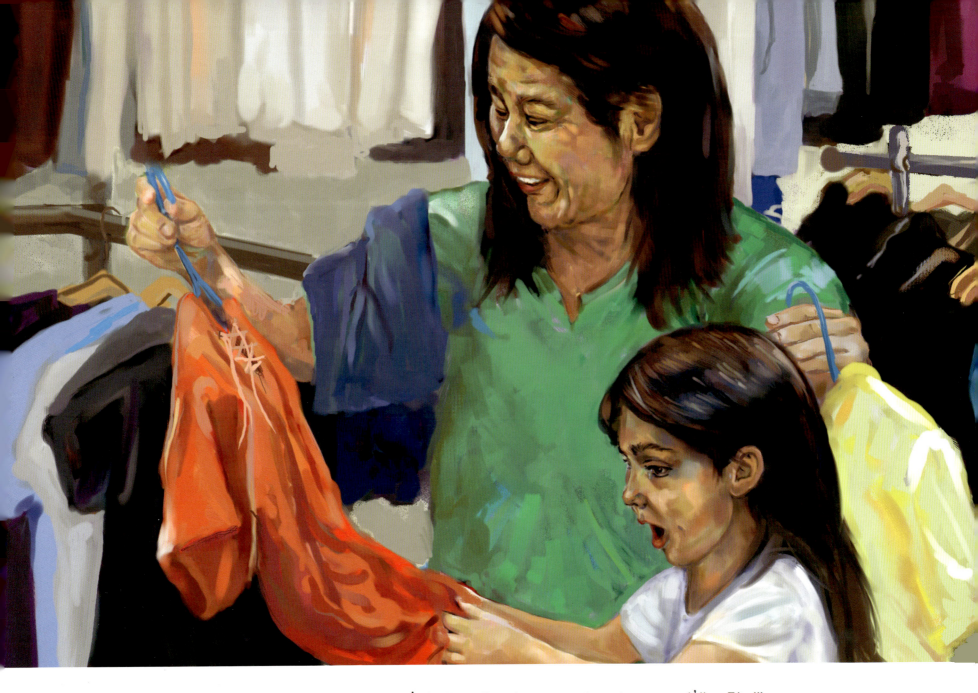

Re Kyé7es m tewens re stektítśe7 ell m clleqelcwes ne stage te m pepelqilc. Phyllis tskwenméysts re stsqeyeken ne stenes re tkwelkwlólse te stektítśe7s welem kitsc. Tsut re newi7s, ta7 me7 sllcwentes wel me7 cketscus e snests te skul.

Re Phyllis tseklem wel neri7 re scketscuses re sitqt, re Phyllis yerí7 re sxeteqsts re sllcwentes re gwellgwelt ell tkwelkwelóĺse te stektítśe7, putens re kyé7es. Lletsqentem te Kyé7es m tsuntmes, "What loves it?" Re Phyllis ell re s7i7llcw te stsmemelt m clleqelcwes ne xqwtsílcten, m ceyects re Kyé7es,

Lu7 seséle te sciláp eytsell kitscwes ne Residential Skul – P̓7ecw re skekwes, tá7a re Phyllis penhen k scweset.s tri7 tek tśilem. Ri7 m tspeqw7uyes te ctsek̓wsten, tsek̓lem es wekúlecwens tḱé7en k t̓7ekwes.

M nexlle7úys re Phyllis le m kitscwes, Re Residential Skul p̓7ecw re swistes, ta7 penhen re Phyllis k swikts t̓ri7 k tsilem.
Wel geygit well siste te estpenllcw te skul es t7eyentem.

Re Phyllis sewens re 7eqwi7cwst.s, tskenem te sq̓7ests neri7 me7 sw7ecs. Tsuntem te eqwi7yewst.s heqen kelles te xetspqiqéṅst te s7itc eytsell me7 pepelq̓ilcwes. Wel tśílem tek wel me7 yews k kelles te xetspqiqéṅst.

Well siste 7ullcwests re stsmemlt, tet7ek te tstalelc wel 7ullcw ne nek̓w7ellcw, neri7 re m k̓ulentmes e stkllentsut.s, m secwsécwmes. Re Phyllis ta7 penhen k swikts k séwllkwe te ts.sicwt tri7 te tśílem. Re Phyllis ta7 k stsuns e skllentes re gwellgwellt ell tkwelkwlóĺse7 te stektítśe7s.

Ḱemell m ḱúlentem te siste. Neneńs le m kectmes te t́ícwell te stsyex te ta7á k sxwexwístes. Well siste 7emut.sts re Phyllis ne tśelcwílep m nikctmes te qewtens. Sulltimcmens le tkwelkwlóĺse te stektít́se7s, kéméll m tsúntem ta7 k stsq́éýs e sllcwentes, Phyllis m tsuns, "Tpelqcictsme, Ta7 ke7 sutens, ri7 ren susten." Ḱemell ta7 kem sq̇elenméntem.

Telri7 te Residential Skul re Phyllis re ta7ús k sxepqenwellens tek stem. Tsukw tucw ri7 re stsmemlt wes re c7eticwes ell re c7illnes. Phyllis tselxemwílcts well sista ta7 k stemstes e tleles, e k7epes, e tsecteylltsus ell e cwemcwemés. Tsukw ne newi7s me7 knucwentsútes, tri7 wel ta7 k swet.s. Ne screpqin re Phyllis ell re s7i7llcw te stsmemlt me7 c7íllen tek pecwt ell ta7 put k pellstsextens te stsíllen.

Ta7 put k sle7es te stsíllen ell re swewll ta7 k sts̓ílems te sqlélten ec te tsc7illenstses mete te Kyé7es. Ne sr7al re Phyllis m tsut kenem me7 te ta7ús re Kyé7es te stskitsens e skwens. M ts̓7úmes ri7 wel 7etic. Ne stmtúmens, ec re seysús ne Kyé7es re ck̓wén̓llqtens ell ec re yéwmes te sqlélten ne setétkwe.

Ne snekw7ésqt, re stsmemlt me7 clleqelc ne xqwtsilcten e snests te tegwn ten skul. Le clleqelcwes ne xqwtsilcten ri7 me7 kectem tek k̓wimememull te tkwelkwléltse te s7uy ell stsq̓yeyken tsecllem te screpqinems. Ne nekus7es telrí7 k tenk̓we7 e tekselus te stsmemlt me7 pell tsoklet ne screpqinems. Xwewéyt te swet me7 t̓7em ne stsq̓yekens k̓emell t̓ucw tsukw k sanwets t̓ekci7 me7 sten.

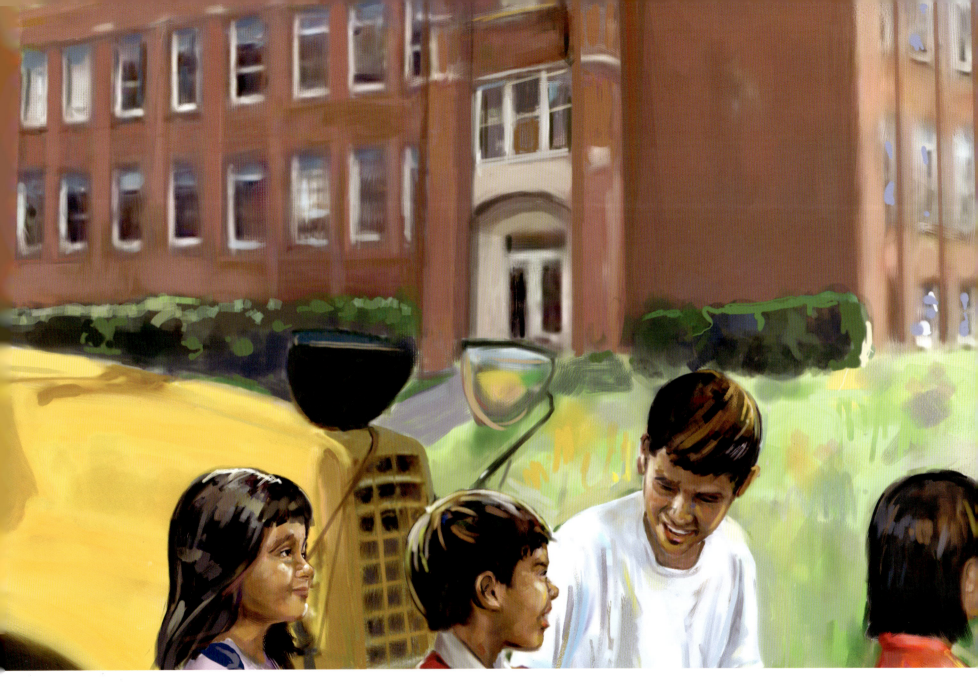

Wel tsilem te tsgweystem te stetéx7em.
Re Phyllis mete 7eq̇wi7ewst.s m clleqelc ne xqwtsilcten. Ne sexwyesq̇t re tskw̓en̓elk ne xqwetsilcten. M ckllilcts 7eq̇wi7yews ne ṫicwell te skul. Phyllis ṫinucw e stnesmens. Ta7 k stselxemstés kenem me7 e sta7us me7 sṫeqwéwsts neri7.

Ne skul re Phyllis mete s7i7llcw te stsmemlt xepqenwens e sqwelteĺtcwes ell e sqẏems, ḱemell ec ey re cwemcwemes, xwexeyt.s re stsmemlt ne Residential Skul lu7 cwempmins re ḱwseltktens.

Te m kwenkwentem te thé7ne we ne tsyemes ell te k̓weselktens. Re lleq̓meltens lu7 tskelklep̓o7sqen te tseqwqin, le7 lu7 te qelmúcw. Ec re tsqwit̓semstses re Phyllis ell ec re tsknucwstses ne s7elkst.s. Tsk̓ulsts e sle7s te sw7ec ne skul.

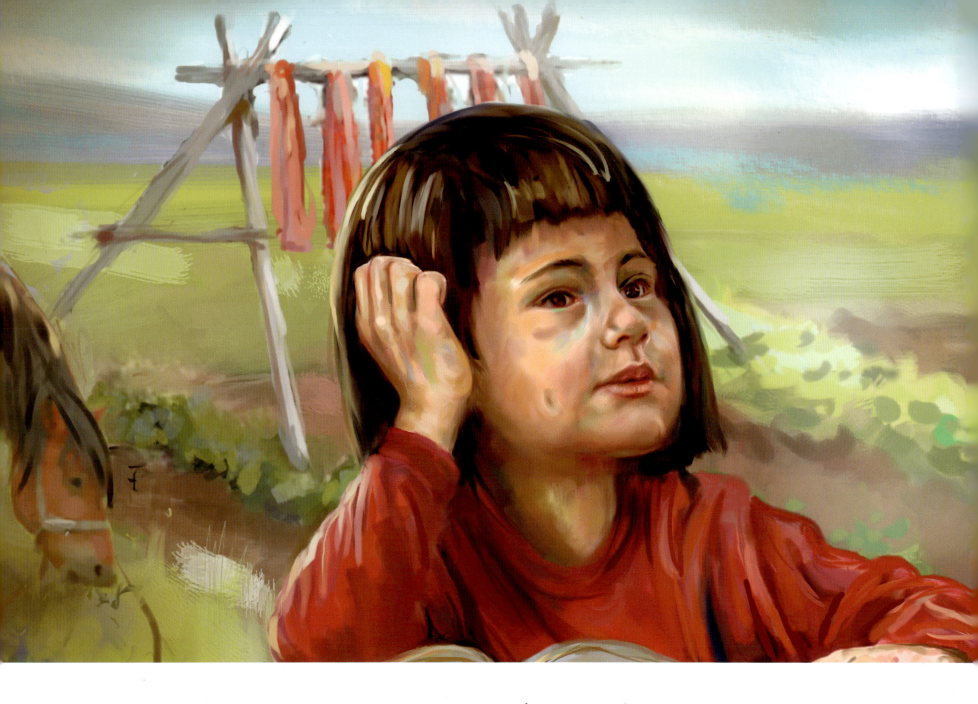

Re Phyllis xwexwístes re llq̓meltens k̓emell ta7 k sts̓ílems te Kyé7es.
M tsut ecenke k kenmes re Kyé7es re m w7ecwes re Phyllis ne skul ne sexwyésqt̓.

Re Phyllis m tscempminsts wes ne mutes ell re ckwenllqtens. Yews ri7 re m sxyens re sitqt penhé7en te pelqilcwes. Ne snekwésqt re m7eyes te spelqilces.
M tseklémes ell m tseklémes.

Re s7i7llcw te stsmemlt ne skul ec re q̓yémes tek spqwpeqwéltcw. K̓emell re stsmemlt ne Residential Skul ta7 k stsq̓ey̓s tri7 e sxílems. Re Phyllis ta7 k stselxemstés kenem me7e re sticwells re stsúwet.stem. Re newí7s ri7 qwnen tek speqwéltcw, ell kenem re stá7es k sten̓cwentem.

Ne cseyséten, ri7 tsilem te xwexwéytes re sqelqéqlemcw ell nxnunxwénxw. Ne screpqín xwexwéyt m seysétwecw. Re Phyllis xepqenwéns es xqetyúle7es ell me7 teqlentes re xqetyúle7ten ne tsrep ell m tspiqwsts re m cwelpepípes.

Re p̓7ecw re sle7s te sitq̓t ri7 re m cketscúses re xqwtsilcten es kwentem re m cwtepes re skul. Re Phyllis kúmtus re stsk̓willcts re 7uq̓wis te smuten̓. Re m kitsentmes re 7eq̓w7yewsts, m cwiselc te xqwtsilcten tek me7 emut ne sequt.s re Phyllis. Nekú7eses ri7 me7 tskwnem tek qwléwe te spepens ne skul.

Re 7eqw7yewsts me7 tsuns, qwnénenk? Re Phyllis m tu7lílmens te estcweltsin te qwléwe. Ḱemell re Phyllis kúmtus re stsectéylltses. M kwens re qwléwe m 7íllenses wel tsilem tek apels. M estcweltsínes tsilem re 7eqw7yewst.s.

Ne xqwtsilcten, ri7 xepqenwéns e setsetsínems. M setsinem, "We are the missions, mighty, mighty missions, everywhere we go, oh, people want to know, oh… who we are… so we tell them, we are the missions…"

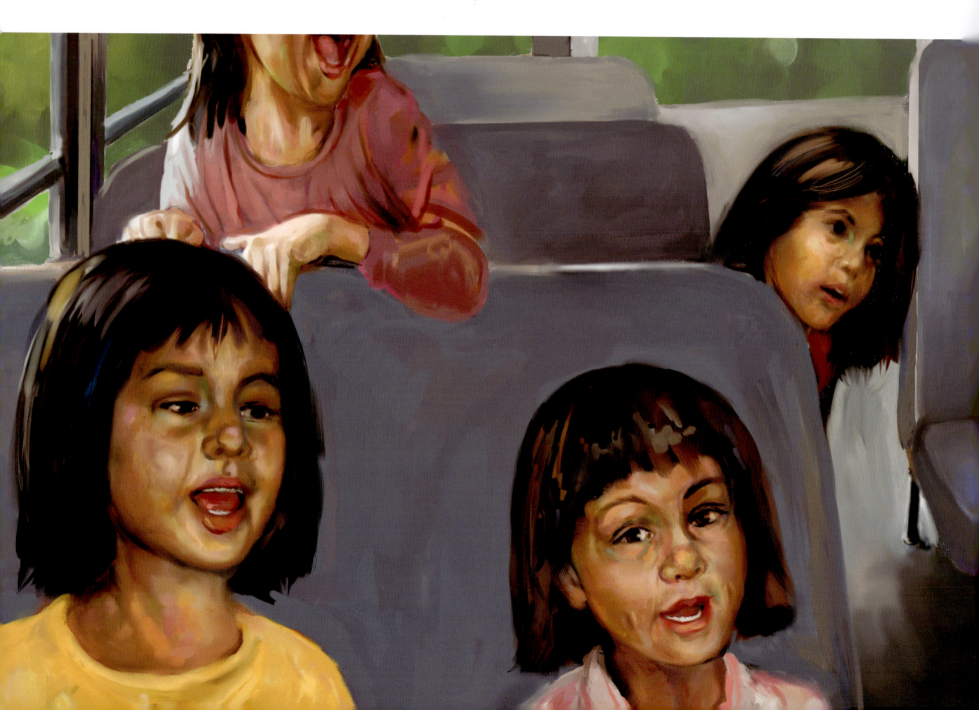

Le m n7ekes re tmicw te sllwélsten, ne s7istk. Yem well sqepts ell cúytsem m sexqelqeltemcwes. Phyllis q7íses e spelqílcs. Ta7 cúytsem k stsut.s e spelqílcs te Residential Skul ell ta7 penhen cúytsem e swikts well ckesksélltse te siste.

Le m kélles te sxetspqíqeṅst, re stage tskitsc e spelq̇entés re Phyllis te mutes ne Xgétṫeṁ. Ts7ecwe7úyes e sw7ecs ṫhé7en k tselxemstémes tek sumecs ell e stsyucwemínstem te qelmúcw.

Ne sexqéḻqeltemc, m mútes ri7 ne Kyé7es. M mútes ri7 ne tsitcw te tselxemstés ell ec re 7elkstés mete Kyé7es ne cḵweṅllqtens. M yeṫelc te Setétkwe e syéwems tek sqlélten ell m 7íllen te sqlélten n screpqín. Cweteméles ri7 ell ta7 cúy̓tsem kem stsuts.s e spelq̓ílcs te Residential Skul.
Yeri7 stsukws.

September 30th- Orange Shirt Day:
Today the residential schools have closed for good.
She and her family learn about and celebrate their culture. Phyllis knows what it means to be Northern Secwépemc, and she is proud of who she is and who her people are.

Each year, on September 30th, many people including Phyllis wear bright orange shirts to honour residential school survivors and their families. Orange Shirt Day kicks off talks about anti racism and bullying at the beginning of the school year.

Phyllis's true story is only one among many. We must listen to these stories, and we must learn from our past. By doing so, we can walk into the future without making the same mistakes again. When we wear our orange shirts on Orange Shirt Day, we reaffirm that every child matters — the children from every nation around the world, the residential school survivors, and the First Nations children who didn't come home.

About the Author:

Phyllis Webstad (nee Jack) is Northern Secwépemc (Shuswap) from the Stswecem'c Xgat'tem First Nation (Canoe Creek Indian Band). She comes from mixed Secwépemc and Irish/French heritage. She was born in Dog Creek and lives in Williams Lake, BC. Phyllis is married, has a son, a stepson, three grandsons and one granddaughter.

Every year, Phyllis and her family camp by the Fraser River near Williams Lake. The old and the young come together to catch and dry fish just like their ancestors did. These are lessons that Phyllis learned as a child. Now, she is proud to teach her grandchildren the ways of her people. Phyllis is a third-generation residential school survivor.

She earned diplomas in Business Administration from the Nicola Valley Institute of Technology and in Accounting from Thompson Rivers University. Phyllis received the 2017 TRU Distinguished Alumni Community Impact Award for her unprecedented impact on local, provincial, national and international communities through the sharing of her orange shirt story.

"This books gives a genuine, serious reflection of a real event, without being angry or sentimental or biased. It flows easily, logically and it's interesting and very relatable, no matter what your childhood experience might be."
Jane Hancock, Principal, Dog Creek Elem/Rural Secondary

When Phyllis Webstad (nee Jack) turned six, she went to the residential school for the first time. On her first day at school, she wore a shiny orange shirt that her Granny had bought for her, but when she got to the school, it was taken away and never returned.
This is the true story of Phyllis and her orange shirt. It is also the story of Orange Shirt Day, an important day of remembrance for all Canadians.

$19.99 + tax

9 781989 122013